The Silent Wounds: Understanding "Type A" Trauma and Healing from Emotional Neglect

By Joycelyn Johnson, LPCC-s, LMHC

Disclaimer: The information provided here is for educational and informational purposes only and is not intended as a substitute for professional mental health advice, diagnosis, or treatment. Although I strive to provide accurate and up-to-date information, this content **<u>should not</u>** be used as a replacement for individual consultation with a licensed mental health professional. If you or someone you know is experiencing a mental health crisis, please contact a qualified mental health provider, call emergency services, or reach out to a crisis hotline - 988.

<u>****PLEASE NOTE**PLEASE NOTE**PLEASE NOTE****</u>

I am not a traditional writer, but I am passionate about using technology to develop and share basic mental health concepts that are accessible to everyone. My goal is to introduce existing foundational ideas that can help people improve their mental health and support the well-being of those they care about. These resources are designed for anyone who wants to learn and grow on their mental health journey.

There is so much I didn't know growing up, and I believe my mother didn't know either—largely because she was in survival mode, especially during my key developmental stages. This lack of knowledge, while understandable, is something I find unacceptable. I believe that understanding must come before action.

The books and materials I create are just the beginning of a learning and healing journey. Once you are exposed to new knowledge, it's impossible to "un-know" it. A seed has been planted, and the growth of that seed depends on how it is nurtured and cared for. My hope is that these tools will plant seeds of awareness, healing, and growth, sparking change that can ripple outward to create healthier individuals, families, and communities.

Table of Contents

Introduction

The Silent Wounds of "Type A" **Trauma**
Trauma is often associated with what *happened* to someone: the painful, disruptive events that leave scars — this is "Type B" trauma. But what about the wounds caused by what *didn't happen*? "Type A" trauma, or absence trauma, is the result of emotional neglect — the absence of love, validation, safety, or connection that a child fundamentally needs to thrive. Unlike physical or emotional abuse, "Type A" trauma does not leave visible marks, making it harder to identify, acknowledge, or address.

Emotional neglect is frequently overlooked or misunderstood because it is invisible. It happens quietly, in homes that may otherwise appear functional, to parents who may have been physically present but emotionally unavailable. There are no dramatic stories or clear events to point to — just a vague sense that something was missing, something essential. This absence is often dismissed by the individual, their family, or society at large, leaving many to question whether their feelings are valid.

The impact of unmet emotional needs in childhood can be profound, lingering far into adulthood. It shapes self-worth, the ability to form and maintain healthy relationships, and the capacity to manage emotions. Chronic feelings of emptiness, self-doubt, perfectionism, and struggles with vulnerability are often rooted in this invisible trauma. The consequences manifest not in dramatic ways but in subtle patterns of behavior that keep individuals disconnected from their true selves and others.

This book was written to shed light on the silent wounds of "Type A" trauma — to give voice to those who have struggled in silence, unsure of what they're even missing. It aims to help readers understand the nature of emotional neglect, recognize its impact, and take actionable steps toward healing. By exploring the grief, the wounds, and the journey to wholeness, this book offers a roadmap for reclaiming the love, validation, and sense of safety that every person deserves.

If you have ever felt unseen, unheard, or unworthy without understanding why, this book is for you. If you have struggled to form meaningful relationships or have carried an unexplainable emptiness, this book is for you. It is time to name the losses, grieve the unmet needs, and begin the process of reparenting yourself. Healing is not about perfection but about progress, and this book will guide you toward a life where your emotional needs are acknowledged, honored, and met.

The journey begins with understanding—understanding what was missing, why it mattered, and how you can heal. Through knowledge, compassion, and actionable tools, you will begin to uncover the invisible scars of "Type A" trauma and take your first steps toward reclaiming wholeness.

Part 1: Understanding "Type A" Trauma

Chapter 1: What is "Type A" Trauma? – "Type A" trauma refers to emotional neglect, defined as the "absence of what should have been" during a child's development. Key developmental needs such as love, validation, structure, and safety are often unmet in these cases. Emotional neglect can occur even in seemingly functional families, making it harder to recognize. Common examples include a lack of emotional support, validation of feelings, or consistent care during childhood.

Chapter 2: The Impact of Unmet Needs – Unmet emotional needs have significant consequences. Emotionally, they can lead to chronic emptiness, low self-esteem, and a struggle to be vulnerable. Physically and neurologically, they can alter brain development and cause chronic stress responses. Socially, "Type A" trauma often results in attachment issues, difficulty forming healthy relationships, and mistrust of others. Its invisible nature often leads society—and individuals themselves—to dismiss its seriousness and impact.

Chapter 3: How "Type A" Trauma Manifests in Adulthood – In adulthood, emotional neglect shapes behaviors such as overachievement, people-pleasing, or avoidance as coping mechanisms. Individuals may struggle with emotional regulation, lack self-awareness, and perpetuate cycles of emotional unavailability in their relationships. Generic case studies highlight how adults unknowingly live with the effects of "Type A" trauma, illustrating its profound influence on emotional, social, and psychological well-being.

Chapter 1: What is "Type A" Trauma?

When we think of trauma, we often imagine events that are overt and unmistakably harmful—abuse, violence, or a sudden, life-altering experience. However, not all trauma is visible, loud, or obvious. "Type A" trauma, also known as emotional neglect, is defined as the *"absence of what should have been"* during a child's development. It is not what happened, but rather what *didn't happen*—the emotional nurturing, care, and connection that every child requires to grow into a healthy, secure adult.

Understanding Emotional Neglect

"Type A" trauma arises when key developmental needs—such as love, validation, structure, and safety—are consistently unmet. Children depend on caregivers not only for physical necessities like food and shelter but also for emotional nourishment. This includes feeling seen, heard, understood, and supported. When these fundamental emotional needs go unmet, the child's sense of self, safety, and connection is deeply affected.

Unlike other forms of trauma, emotional neglect is often subtle and unintentional. It can occur even in seemingly "functional" families where parents provide financial stability, meet physical needs, and appear outwardly caring. Despite appearances, emotional neglect occurs when caregivers fail to offer consistent emotional presence, validation, or responsiveness to their child's feelings and experiences.

Key Developmental Needs

During childhood, emotional and psychological growth depends on the fulfillment of several core needs:

1. **Love**: Children need to feel loved unconditionally. Affection, warmth, and emotional connection lay the foundation for self-worth and trust in relationships.
2. **Validation**: Children need their thoughts, feelings, and experiences to be acknowledged and affirmed. This helps

them develop a sense of confidence, self-awareness, and emotional literacy.
3. **Structure**: Consistent routines, boundaries, and guidance create a sense of safety and predictability. Without structure, children may feel insecure or uncertain about how to navigate the world.
4. **Safety**: Emotional safety allows children to express themselves without fear of judgment, rejection, or punishment. It fosters trust, vulnerability, and a sense of belonging.

When any of these needs are chronically unmet, children grow up with gaps in their emotional development that follow them into adulthood.

Emotional Neglect in "Functional" Families
"Type A" trauma can be particularly difficult to identify because it often occurs in families that appear "normal" on the surface. Parents may provide a stable home, work hard to meet physical needs, and even express love in their own way. However, emotional neglect is not about intent—it is about the child's *experience*.

For example:
- A child who shares their sadness or frustration may be dismissed with phrases like *"You're fine,"* or *"Stop crying, it's not a big deal."*
- A parent may be physically present but emotionally distant—unresponsive to their child's needs for comfort, attention, or connection.
- Children may be praised for achievements but ignored when expressing fear, anger, or sadness.
- Busy or overwhelmed parents may unintentionally fail to provide guidance, support, or consistent care, leaving the child to navigate challenges alone.

In these families, the absence of emotional nurturing is often overlooked because it does not involve overt harm or abuse. As a result, many adults who experienced "Type A" trauma struggle to recognize their upbringing as neglectful, saying things like, *"My parents did the best they could,"* or *"I had a roof over my head, so what do I have to complain about?"*

Common Examples of Emotional Neglect
The following examples illustrate how emotional neglect can manifest during childhood:

- **Feelings Invalidated**: A child is repeatedly told to "toughen up" or "stop being dramatic" when expressing emotions.
- **Lack of Emotional Support**: When facing challenges, the child receives little to no comfort, guidance, or reassurance.
- **Inconsistent Care**: Caregivers may be distracted, emotionally distant, or unavailable due to their own stress, mental health issues, or life circumstances.
- **Achievement Over Connection**: A parent focuses primarily on the child's accomplishments, leaving little room to acknowledge emotional struggles or needs.
- **Absence of Boundaries**: Without clear routines or structure, children feel unsafe, unsupported, or uncertain about expectations.

Why Emotional Neglect is Hard to Recognize
Because "Type A" trauma involves the *absence* of emotional care rather than the presence of harmful actions, it often goes unnoticed. Unlike abuse, there are no clear events to point to — no physical wounds, harsh words, or explosive incidents. Instead, the harm lies in what *wasn't given* and the quiet emptiness that remains.

Many adults dismiss their emotional neglect because they compare their experiences to others who faced overt trauma. Thoughts like, *"Other people had it so much worse,"* or *"I shouldn't complain; I was never hit or abused,"* minimize their own pain and delay the process of understanding and healing.

However, emotional neglect is a profound and valid form of trauma. Its impact is real, even if it is invisible. The absence of love, validation, structure, and safety in childhood leaves children feeling unseen, unworthy, and emotionally adrift. These wounds remain beneath the surface, influencing how they relate to themselves and others for years to come.

Moving Forward
Recognizing "Type A" trauma is the first step toward healing. By understanding that emotional neglect is real and its effects are significant, we begin to validate our experiences and acknowledge the gaps left by unmet needs. Emotional neglect may not leave visible scars, but its impact on emotional, social, and psychological well-being is profound.

In the chapters that follow, we will explore how the absence of emotional nurturing shapes behaviors, emotions, and relationships in adulthood. By uncovering the invisible wounds of "Type A" trauma, we can begin the journey toward healing, wholeness, and emotional fulfillment.

Chapter 2: The Impact of Unmet Needs

The absence of emotional nurturing during childhood — known as "Type A" trauma — can leave profound and lasting scars. Unlike overt trauma, emotional neglect is subtle, making it harder to identify and understand. Yet, its impact on emotional, physical, and social well-being is undeniable. The unmet needs of love, validation, structure, and safety shape how individuals see themselves, relate to others, and navigate the world.

Emotional Consequences: Chronic Emptiness, Low Self-Esteem, and Vulnerability

When emotional needs are consistently ignored, children internalize a sense of unworthiness. Over time, this develops into persistent feelings of emptiness — a void that seems impossible to fill. Adults who experienced emotional neglect may struggle with:

1. **Chronic Emptiness** This emotional void manifests as a deep, lingering sense that something is "missing," even when life appears to be going well. Individuals often try to fill this emptiness with external distractions, such as work, achievements, or unhealthy coping mechanisms like overeating, overworking, or substance use. Despite these efforts, the emptiness persists because the root need — emotional connection — remains unmet.

2. **Low Self-Esteem** When a child's emotions and experiences are invalidated, they learn to question their worth. In adulthood, this often translates into a harsh inner critic and a belief that they are unlovable or inadequate. People may shy away from opportunities or relationships, fearing they will not measure up or deserve the happiness they seek.

3. **Struggle with Vulnerability** Emotional neglect teaches children to suppress their feelings and avoid vulnerability as a form of self-protection. As adults, they may find it incredibly difficult to open up, even with those they care about. Vulnerability feels risky, as it

exposes the individual to potential rejection, criticism, or further neglect. This struggle often keeps them disconnected and isolated, even within their closest relationships.

Physical and Neurological Effects: The Brain Under Stress
Unmet emotional needs do not just affect mental health — they also have physical and neurological consequences. During childhood, consistent emotional connection and validation help regulate a child's stress response system. Without this, the body remains in a prolonged state of stress, which can lead to:

1. **Chronic Stress Responses** The nervous system becomes overactive, leaving individuals in a near-constant state of fight-or-flight. This can result in physical symptoms like fatigue, muscle tension, digestive issues, and headaches. Over time, chronic stress contributes to conditions such as high blood pressure, cardiovascular issues, and immune system dysfunction.

2. **Changes in Brain Development** Emotional neglect during critical developmental years can alter brain structure and function, particularly in areas responsible for emotional regulation, decision-making, and connection. The brain learns to adapt to emotional absence by suppressing feelings or avoiding connection, which can affect mental health and coping abilities well into adulthood.

3. **Heightened Sensitivity or Numbness** Some adults develop a hyper-sensitivity to stress or conflict, while others experience emotional numbness, struggling to feel anything at all. These responses are survival mechanisms, ways the brain learned to adapt to a lack of nurturing and safety.

Social Challenges: Attachment Issues, Relationship Struggles, and Mistrust
The impact of "Type A" trauma extends deeply into social and relational dynamics. Growing up without emotional support

teaches children that relationships are unsafe, unreliable, or not worth pursuing. In adulthood, this often manifests as:

1. **Attachment Issues** Emotional neglect disrupts the natural process of developing secure attachments. Adults may struggle to form meaningful connections because they did not learn how to trust, express emotions, or depend on others in healthy ways. Instead, they may experience:
   a. **Avoidant attachment**: Keeping others at a distance to avoid vulnerability.
   b. **Anxious attachment**: Clinging to relationships out of fear of abandonment.
   c. **Disorganized attachment**: A mix of avoidance and anxiety, leaving individuals unsure of how to connect.

2. **Difficulty Forming Healthy Relationships** Unmet emotional needs often result in relational patterns that mirror childhood experiences. Adults may enter relationships where their needs continue to go unmet or feel drawn to emotionally unavailable partners.

   Alternatively, they may avoid relationships altogether, fearing rejection or repeating painful experiences.

3. **Mistrust of Others** At its core, emotional neglect teaches individuals that others cannot be relied upon for support or care. This can lead to deep mistrust, even in the presence of kind and supportive people. Adults may interpret emotional closeness as a threat and unconsciously push others away, reinforcing feelings of isolation.

The Invisible Nature of "Type A" Trauma
One of the most challenging aspects of "Type A" trauma is its invisibility. Because emotional neglect is the *absence* of something rather than a visible act, society—and even

individuals themselves — often dismiss its significance. Adults may say, *"I had a roof over my head and food on the table; I had no reason to feel neglected."* While their physical needs were met, their emotional needs were not, and this unacknowledged pain can lead to confusion, shame, and self-blame.

The subtlety of emotional neglect makes it easy to overlook, but its impact is no less real. Recognizing that emotional absence has long-term consequences is a vital step toward healing. Naming this trauma helps individuals make sense of their struggles and begin to untangle the patterns it has created in their lives.

Moving Forward
The consequences of unmet emotional needs are far-reaching, affecting emotional health, physical well-being, and relationships. Yet, understanding the impact of "Type A" trauma is also empowering. By identifying these effects, individuals can begin to address the void left by emotional neglect and take the first steps toward healing. Though the wounds may be invisible, their impact is profound — and so is the potential for growth, transformation, and emotional fulfillment.

Chapter 3: How "Type A" Trauma Manifests in Adulthood

The effects of emotional neglect, or "Type A" trauma, often follow individuals into adulthood, shaping behaviors, emotional patterns, and relationships in ways they may not fully recognize. Though it may seem invisible, the absence of key emotional needs during childhood — such as love, validation, structure, and safety — leaves a lasting imprint that influences how adults engage with themselves, others, and the world around them.

Coping Mechanisms: Overachievement, People-Pleasing, and Avoidance

For many adults who experienced emotional neglect, coping often comes in the form of behaviors that attempt to earn validation or protect against further pain. These behaviors are usually developed unconsciously during childhood and become ingrained habits:

1. **Overachievement** – Adults with "Type A" trauma may throw themselves into work, education, or personal goals to prove their worth. Overachievement becomes a way to compensate for the validation they never received as children. This constant striving for external success often leads to burnout, chronic stress, and dissatisfaction because achievements rarely fill the emotional void.
2. **People-Pleasing** – People-pleasing is another common pattern. Adults may feel compelled to meet others' needs, often at the expense of their own. Seeking approval becomes a way to feel valued and avoid rejection. However, this behavior often results in an inability to set boundaries, leaving individuals feeling resentful, drained, and unseen.
3. **Avoidance** – Some adults adopt avoidance as a defense mechanism to shield themselves from emotional discomfort. This may involve avoiding intimate relationships, sidestepping difficult emotions, or disengaging from situations that require vulnerability.

While avoidance may offer short-term relief, it isolates individuals and perpetuates feelings of emptiness and disconnection.

Struggles with Emotional Regulation and Self-Awareness
One of the most profound effects of "Type A" trauma is difficulty with emotional regulation. Because their emotional needs were dismissed or overlooked in childhood, adults may struggle to identify and manage their emotions. Feelings like anger, sadness, or fear may be suppressed or expressed in extreme ways, leading to internal confusion and instability.

Without the experience of being guided through emotional challenges as children, adults often lack self-awareness. They may not understand why they react the way they do or why certain situations trigger intense emotional responses. This disconnect from their own feelings makes it difficult to resolve conflicts or cultivate self-compassion.

Emotional Unavailability in Relationships
The cycle of emotional neglect often repeats itself in adult relationships. Individuals who grew up without emotional nurturing may struggle to provide it to their partners, friends, or children. Emotional unavailability can manifest as:

- Difficulty expressing feelings or needs.
- A fear of vulnerability, leading to superficial or guarded relationships.
- Seeking partners who are similarly unavailable, recreating familiar patterns.

For example, an adult may find themselves repeatedly in relationships where their emotional needs go unmet. They may also struggle to recognize healthy, supportive partners because emotional neglect has shaped their understanding of love and connection.

<h1 style="text-align:center">Case Studies: Living with "Type A" Trauma</h1>

To illustrate the real-world impact of "Type A" trauma, consider the following scenarios:

- **Case Study 1: The Overachiever** – Jane, a 35-year-old marketing professional, thrives in her career. She works late nights, volunteers for extra projects, and consistently wins awards for her performance. Yet, despite her success, Jane feels empty and unfulfilled. She avoids deep relationships and has trouble understanding her constant need to prove herself. Jane's drive for achievement masks the lingering pain of growing up in a home where her feelings were dismissed and her worth was tied to accomplishments.

- **Case Study 2: The People-Pleaser** – Michael, a 40-year-old father of two, struggles to say "no" to anyone. Whether at work, with friends, or at home, he feels responsible for making others happy. Michael's people-pleasing behavior stems from a childhood where he was praised for being "easygoing" and never causing trouble. Now, as an adult, he finds it difficult to set boundaries, leading to exhaustion and resentment.

- **Case Study 3: The Avoidant** – Sarah, a 28-year-old artist, has a history of short-lived relationships. She pushes people away when they get too close, fearing judgment and rejection. Growing up in a household where emotions were ignored, Sarah learned to rely solely on herself and shut others out. While her independence protects her from vulnerability, it also prevents her from experiencing genuine connection.

The Profound Influence on Well-Being
The long-term effects of "Type A" trauma are not always obvious, but they influence every aspect of an individual's life — emotionally, socially, and psychologically. Adults may unknowingly carry the weight of unmet needs, feeling a persistent sense of emptiness, disconnection, or "something missing." This often leads to struggles with relationships, self-worth, and overall life satisfaction.

Recognizing how "Type A" trauma manifests in adulthood is a crucial step toward healing. By identifying these patterns, individuals can begin to understand their behaviors, nurture their emotional needs, and break free from cycles of neglect. Though the wounds of emotional neglect run deep, awareness and compassion can create space for growth, healing, and transformation.

Part 2: Grieving the Losses of "Type A" Trauma

Chapter 4: Naming the Losses – Healing from "Type A" trauma begins with identifying what was missing during childhood, such as affection, validation, guidance, and support. Acknowledging the grief of not having a "normal, healthy" childhood is essential for healing. Naming these losses helps individuals validate their experiences and serves as a critical first step toward recovery.

Chapter 5: Breaking the Silence – Emotional neglect often brings feelings of shame and guilt, making it difficult to talk about. Validating one's experiences without minimizing them is key to breaking this silence. Overcoming societal and cultural stigmas around emotional neglect empowers individuals to embrace their truth and begin the healing process.

Chapter 6: Allowing Yourself to Grieve – Mourning the childhood, you didn't have is a necessary part of healing. Grief is not the same as self-pity but an important step in processing unresolved emotions. Tools such as journaling, mindfulness, play, visualization, and self-reflection exercises can guide individuals in exploring and expressing their grief, facilitating emotional growth and release.

Chapter 4: Naming the Losses

Healing from "Type A" trauma—emotional neglect—requires more than recognizing its presence; it begins with naming what was missing. The emotional absence that defines "Type A" trauma often leaves a void, yet it can feel intangible or difficult to pinpoint. Identifying these losses is the first step toward understanding the impact of emotional neglect and validating your experiences. By acknowledging the grief of not having a "normal, healthy" childhood, you lay the foundation for true healing.

Identifying What Was Missing
During childhood, every person has fundamental emotional needs: affection, validation, guidance, and support. When these needs go unmet, the result is often an internal sense of emptiness and confusion. While parents may have provided physical necessities—food, shelter, and education—emotional neglect arises when they fail to meet the *unseen* needs of the heart and mind.

To begin naming the losses, consider the following key emotional needs:

1. **Affection** – Affection provides children with a sense of love and belonging. It includes physical expressions of care, like hugs and comforting touch, as well as verbal affirmations such as *"I love you,"* or *"I'm proud of you."* When affection is absent, children may grow up feeling unworthy of love or connection.
2. **Validation** – Validation means having your emotions, experiences, and thoughts acknowledged and affirmed. Children need to hear that their feelings are real and acceptable. When caregivers dismiss emotions with phrases like *"Stop crying,"* or *"You're being dramatic,"* children internalize the message that their emotions are unimportant or wrong.

3. **Guidance** – Guidance provides children with the tools to navigate life's challenges. It includes teaching emotional regulation, offering advice during struggles, and modeling healthy relationships. When this guidance is lacking, children are left to figure things out on their own, leading to feelings of insecurity and overwhelm.
4. **Support** – Support is the consistent emotional presence of a caregiver who shows up during both successes and failures. Without this safety net, children may feel alone in their experiences, learning to suppress their needs to avoid burdening others.

Acknowledging the Grief

Naming these losses brings up a natural and necessary emotion: grief. Grief is the acknowledgment of what *should have been* but wasn't—the love you didn't receive, the safety you never felt, and the support you needed but couldn't rely on. This can be one of the most challenging steps in the healing process because it requires facing what was missing and allowing yourself to feel the sadness, anger, or longing that may arise.

It's common to resist this grief. You might think:

- *"It wasn't that bad; other people had it worse."*
- *"My parents did their best. I shouldn't blame them."*
- *"There's no point in dwelling on the past."*

However, grief is not about assigning blame or staying stuck. It's about honoring your truth and recognizing the losses you experienced. By grieving, you validate your pain and create space for healing. Ignoring this step often leads to suppression, where unresolved emotions continue to influence your thoughts, behaviors, and relationships in adulthood.

Why Naming the Losses Matters

Naming the losses of emotional neglect serves a critical purpose: it gives form to the formless. The absence of emotional care can feel vague or unrecognizable, leaving individuals wondering why they struggle with feelings of emptiness, insecurity, or disconnection. Naming what was missing allows you to:

- **Connect the Dots**: Understanding the root of your struggles helps you make sense of patterns in your life, such as people-pleasing, avoidance, or emotional numbness.
- **Validate Your Experiences**: Acknowledging the losses helps you affirm that your pain is real and deserving of care, even if it isn't tied to obvious events or actions.
- **Begin Healing**: Naming the losses is the first step in reclaiming what was absent. You cannot heal what you do not recognize.

Reflecting on Your Losses
Reflecting on what was missing can feel overwhelming at first. It's important to approach this step with compassion, patience, and gentleness.

Here are a few questions to guide your reflection:

1. What emotional needs did I not receive as a child?
2. How did I feel when my emotions were dismissed or ignored?
3. What memories stand out when I think of feeling unseen, unheard, or unsupported?
4. What did I need most from my caregivers that I didn't get?

Writing these reflections in a journal can be a powerful way to explore your experiences. You may also choose to visualize yourself as a child and imagine what you would have wanted to hear or feel in those moments.

Embracing the Healing Process
Naming the losses is not about blaming your caregivers or dwelling in the past. It is about giving yourself permission to grieve so you can move forward. Emotional neglect often

perpetuates silence and minimization, but by speaking your truth—first to yourself—you break that cycle.

Allow yourself to feel the sadness or anger that may arise as you reflect on what was missing. These emotions are not signs of weakness; they are necessary parts of the healing process. By naming your losses, you take a courageous step toward reclaiming your emotional health and well-being.

Moving Forward
The losses of emotional neglect are real, even if they are invisible. By identifying what was absent—whether it was affection, validation, guidance, or support—you begin to validate your experiences and your pain. Grief, while difficult, opens the door to growth, healing, and the possibility of reclaiming what was lost.

You may not be able to change the past, but you have the power to honor your story, grieve your losses, and build the emotional connections you deserve in the present and future. This step is not the end of your journey—it is the beginning of true recovery.

Chapter 5: Breaking the Silence

For those who experienced emotional neglect, silence often becomes the default response. The absence of emotional nurturing during childhood is rarely acknowledged, leaving individuals with feelings of shame, guilt, and confusion about their experiences. Breaking this silence is a critical step in the healing process, but it requires courage, validation, and a willingness to challenge societal and cultural stigmas surrounding emotional neglect.

The Weight of Silence

Emotional neglect is often invisible, making it difficult for individuals to recognize or articulate their pain. Unlike physical abuse or other overt traumas, there is nothing "visible" to point to — no specific events, injuries, or confrontations. This invisibility creates an internal conflict:

1. *"Why do I feel this way when nothing 'bad' happened to me?"*
2. *"Other people had it worse; I shouldn't complain."*
3. *"If I talk about this, no one will believe me."*

This uncertainty leads to a cycle of silence, where individuals bury their pain, dismiss their experiences, and avoid conversations about their childhood. Yet beneath the silence, the wounds of emotional neglect remain, quietly shaping behaviors, emotions, and relationships.

The longer the silence persists, the heavier the burden becomes. Unspoken pain can manifest as chronic emptiness, resentment, low self-worth, or struggles with trust and connection. Breaking the silence is not about blaming the past but about freeing yourself from its hold and reclaiming your voice.

Shame and Guilt: The Barriers to Speaking Up

Two emotions often prevent individuals from acknowledging emotional neglect: **shame** and **guilt**.

1. **Shame**: Shame whispers that something is fundamentally wrong with you. It tells you that if your emotional needs weren't met, it must be because you were unlovable, unworthy, or not "good enough." This deeply ingrained belief keeps individuals silent, as the act of speaking up feels like exposing an unacceptable flaw.
2. **Guilt**: Guilt stems from minimizing your experiences or fearing that acknowledging emotional neglect will hurt or dishonor your caregivers. Thoughts like *"My parents did their best,"* or *"They worked hard; I have no right to complain,"* reinforce the silence.

It's important to remember that validating your experiences does not mean blaming others. Emotional neglect is often unintentional and stems from generational patterns, cultural expectations, or a caregiver's own struggles. Breaking the silence is not about casting blame — it's about honoring your truth and beginning to heal.

The Power of Validation
The first step in breaking the silence is validating your experiences without minimizing them. Emotional neglect may not leave visible scars, but its impact is real and profound. Your feelings of emptiness, sadness, or disconnection are valid, even if they are hard to explain.

1. **Name Your Truth**: Acknowledge that your emotional needs were not met, and this has shaped your life. Statements like *"I needed love, validation, and support, but I didn't receive it,"* can be powerful affirmations of your experience.
2. **Challenge Minimization**: Avoid downplaying your pain with thoughts like, *"It wasn't that bad,"* or *"I don't deserve to feel this way."* Your emotions are valid because they are *yours.*
3. **Allow Yourself to Feel**: Give yourself permission to grieve what was missing and recognize that doing so is not weakness — it is healing.

When you validate your own experiences, you free yourself from shame and create space for growth. Speaking your truth, even quietly to yourself at first, is an act of courage and self-compassion.

Overcoming Societal and Cultural Stigmas
Society often dismisses the impact of emotional neglect, prioritizing physical care over emotional well-being. Statements like *"You had a roof over your head,"* or *"Your parents worked hard for you,"* can make it difficult to acknowledge the emotional void you experienced.

Cultural beliefs may reinforce this silence further. In some families or communities, emotions are seen as a sign of weakness, and speaking about emotional needs is discouraged. Breaking free from these stigmas requires challenging deeply ingrained messages and embracing the importance of emotional health.

- **Redefine Strength**: True strength is not suppressing emotions but facing them with courage. Acknowledging your pain is a powerful act of resilience.
- **Educate Yourself and Others**: Understanding the impact of emotional neglect helps you validate your experiences and communicate its significance to others.
- **Seek Safe Spaces**: Surround yourself with individuals, communities, or professionals who honor emotional truth and understand the importance of healing.

Overcoming societal and cultural stigmas allows you to reclaim your voice and redefine what it means to be seen, heard, and valued.

The Healing Power of Breaking the Silence
When you speak your truth — whether through journaling, therapy, or trusted relationships — you begin to release the

weight of unspoken pain. Breaking the silence is an act of self-empowerment.

It allows you to:

- Acknowledge and validate your experiences.
- Challenge shame, guilt, and societal messages that dismiss your pain.
- Begin the process of emotional healing and self-compassion.

Sharing your story also helps others. Emotional neglect is far more common than most people realize, yet it remains hidden behind closed doors and unspoken words. By breaking your silence, you inspire others to examine their experiences, validate their emotions, and pursue healing.

Moving Forward
Breaking the silence is not a single moment but an ongoing process. Start small—acknowledge your truth to yourself, write about your experiences, or share them with someone you trust. Every step you take is a step toward freedom, healing, and emotional connection.

You are not alone in this journey. Your experiences matter, your emotions are valid, and your voice deserves to be heard. By embracing your truth, you release the hold of shame and silence and create space for healing, growth, and wholeness.

Breaking the silence is not just about speaking—it's about reclaiming your right to be seen, valued, and emotionally alive. Your story matters, and it is never too late to begin the healing process.

Chapter 6: Allowing Yourself to Grieve

The process of healing from "Type A" trauma—emotional neglect—requires more than understanding what was missing. It requires creating space to grieve. Mourning the childhood, you didn't have is an essential step toward emotional healing and wholeness. While grief may feel uncomfortable or even unnecessary, it allows you to process unresolved emotions, release pain, and move forward with greater clarity and self-compassion.

The Role of Grief in Healing

Grief is a natural response to loss, and for those who experienced emotional neglect, the loss is often intangible. You may not have lost a person or possession, but you lost what *should have been*—love, validation, emotional safety, and consistent care. Grieving the absence of these fundamental needs helps you acknowledge the pain you carry instead of suppressing it.

It is important to recognize that grief is *not self-pity*. Self-pity keeps you stuck, reinforcing a sense of helplessness. Grief, on the other hand, is an act of courage. It is a process of honoring your pain, validating your experiences, and allowing yourself to feel so you can begin to heal.

Why Mourning Matters

Many adults with "Type A" trauma hesitate to grieve. Thoughts like *"It wasn't that bad,"* or *"I don't want to blame my parents,"* often get in the way. However, grieving does not mean assigning blame or dwelling on the past—it means:

- **Recognizing your truth**: Acknowledging that your needs were not met and that it had a real impact.
- **Validating your emotions**: Allowing yourself to feel sadness, anger, or disappointment without judgment.
- **Releasing suppressed pain**: Giving yourself permission to express emotions you may have buried for years.

- **Creating space for growth**: Once the pain is acknowledged and processed, you can begin to rebuild from a place of awareness and compassion.

Grief gives you the freedom to let go of old wounds, step out of patterns shaped by emotional neglect, and move toward a healthier, more fulfilling life.

Tools to Explore and Express Grief
The process of grieving is deeply personal, but certain tools and exercises can guide you through it. These practices help you connect with your emotions, process them safely, and honor the childhood you didn't have.

1. Journaling - Writing allows you to express thoughts and feelings that may be difficult to verbalize. Journaling creates a safe space to reflect on your childhood, name your losses, and explore the emotions that arise.

Prompt Examples:
- "What did I need as a child that I didn't receive?"
- "How does it feel to acknowledge those unmet needs now?"
- "What would I say to my younger self to offer comfort and validation?"

Allow yourself to write freely, without censoring or judging your emotions. The goal is to release what you've been holding onto.

2. Mindfulness - Mindfulness practices help you stay present as you process difficult emotions. Grief often brings up intense feelings—sadness, anger, longing—but mindfulness teaches you to observe these emotions without becoming overwhelmed.

Exercise:
- Sit in a quiet space and focus on your breath.
- When emotions arise, name them gently: *"This is sadness,"* or *"This is anger."*

- Remind yourself: *"It's okay to feel this."*
- Breathe deeply as you allow the feelings to pass through you like waves.

Mindfulness helps you sit with your grief instead of avoiding or suppressing it.

3. Visualization - Visualization can be a powerful tool for connecting with your inner child and processing grief. It allows you to imagine offering comfort and care to the child you once were.

Exercise:
- Close your eyes and imagine yourself as a child — see their face, body language, and emotions.
- Picture your "adult self" sitting beside them, offering love, understanding, and support.
- Speak comforting words: *"You are loved. You are enough. I'm here for you now."*

This practice helps heal the part of you that felt unseen or unloved, replacing pain with compassion.

4. Play and Creativity - Emotional neglect often forces children to grow up too quickly, leaving little room for joy, exploration, and play. Reclaiming these experiences in adulthood is an act of self-healing.

Ideas for Play:
- Engage in activities that bring you joy, such as painting, dancing, playing games, or spending time in nature.
- Allow yourself to experience fun and freedom without guilt.

Play reconnects you with your inner child, reminding you that you deserve lightness and happiness.

5. Self-Reflection Exercises - Guided self-reflection allows you to deepen your understanding of your grief and track your healing journey.

Exercise: Write a letter to your childhood self.
- Acknowledge what they went through.
- Express love, validation, and comfort.
- Offer reassurance that they are now safe and supported.

Rereading this letter can be a source of healing and self-compassion, especially during moments when grief feels heavy.

Embracing the Process of Grief
Grieving is not linear. Some days, the sadness may feel overwhelming; on other days, it may feel distant. Allow yourself to move through this process at your own pace, honoring where you are without judgment.

Be patient with yourself and remember that grief is a natural, necessary step in healing from "Type A" trauma. Each tear shed, word written, or feeling expressed brings you closer to release and emotional freedom.

Moving Forward
Allowing yourself to grieve does not mean erasing the past or dismissing what you endured. Instead, it means acknowledging your pain with compassion and care. Mourning the childhood, you didn't have is a courageous act — one that makes space for growth, healing, and transformation.

By embracing tools like journaling, mindfulness, play, visualization, and self-reflection, you give yourself permission to process what was lost and reclaim what can still be found: a sense of wholeness, emotional connection, and self-love.

You cannot change the past, but you can honor your story, heal your wounds, and create a future where you are seen, heard, and deeply valued. Grief is not the end of your journey — it is the bridge to a new beginning.

Chapter 7: Reparenting Yourself – Reparenting involves caring for your inner child by providing the love, validation, and structure you missed in childhood. Practical strategies include practicing self-compassion, establishing routines that create safety and structure, and creating nurturing self-care rituals. These approaches help meet your own emotional needs and foster healing.

Chapter 8: Rebuilding Emotional Regulation – Addressing emotional wounds requires learning to recognize, express, and manage emotions. Tools for emotional literacy and techniques like mindfulness and grounding exercises help manage overwhelming feelings. Therapy plays a critical role in supporting deep emotional healing, offering guidance in rebuilding emotional stability.

Chapter 9: Building Healthy Relationships – Healthy relationships are essential for recovery. Overcoming trust issues and the fear of vulnerability is key to forming genuine connections. Learning to set and maintain boundaries creates space for emotional safety. Cultivating reciprocal relationships ensures that emotional needs are met in a balanced and fulfilling way.

Chapter 7: Reparenting Yourself

Healing from "Type A" trauma requires more than acknowledging the emotional neglect you experienced—it involves actively nurturing the parts of yourself that were left unseen and unmet. This process, known as **reparenting**, allows you to care for your inner child by providing the love, validation, and structure you didn't receive in childhood. By learning to meet your own emotional needs with compassion and intention, you create a path toward deep, lasting healing.

What Does It Mean to Reparent Yourself?
Reparenting is the act of becoming the caregiver you needed as a child. It is not about erasing the past but about filling in the gaps left by emotional neglect.

It involves consciously providing:

1. **Love**: Unconditional acceptance and care for yourself.
2. **Validation**: Acknowledging your emotions and experiences as real and important.
3. **Structure**: Creating routines and boundaries that provide safety and consistency.
4. **Nurturing**: Offering yourself comfort, encouragement, and the space to grow.

Reparenting is an act of self-empowerment. It allows you to step into the role of a supportive caregiver for your inner child—guiding them toward healing, connection, and security.

Connecting with Your Inner Child
At the core of reparenting is the idea of connecting with your *inner child*. Your inner child represents the part of you that experienced emotional neglect, held unspoken pain, and learned to suppress its needs. By acknowledging and caring for your inner child, you begin to heal those old wounds.

How to Connect with Your Inner Child:

- **Visualization**: Close your eyes and picture yourself as a child. Notice their body language, facial expression, and emotions. Imagine sitting with them, offering love and reassurance. Speak comforting words like:
  - *"I see you. I love you. You are not alone."*
  - *"Your feelings matter, and I'm here to care for you."*
- **Writing Letters**: Write a letter to your younger self, offering validation and compassion. Acknowledge their pain and remind them of their worth.
- **Ask What You Need**: Reflect on what you wish you had heard or experienced as a child. What did you need to feel safe, seen, or loved? Now, find ways to give that to yourself in the present.

These practices help reconnect you with the parts of yourself that need nurturing and begin to build a sense of emotional safety.

Practical Strategies for Reparenting Yourself

1. Practicing Self-Compassion - Self-compassion is the foundation of reparenting. It involves treating yourself with the same kindness and understanding that a loving caregiver would provide. Many adults who experienced emotional neglect are harsh critics of themselves, repeating the invalidation they received in childhood. Reparenting requires replacing that inner critic with an inner nurturer.

Ways to Practice Self-Compassion:

- **Speak to Yourself Kindly**: When you make a mistake, replace self-criticism with gentle encouragement. For example, say: *"It's okay to struggle. I'm proud of how hard I'm trying."*
- **Acknowledge Your Pain**: Validate your emotions instead of dismissing them. Remind yourself: *"It makes sense that I feel this way. My feelings are real, and they matter."*

- **Practice Self-Soothing**: When you feel overwhelmed, comfort yourself as you would a child. Wrap yourself in a blanket, listen to calming music, or repeat soothing affirmations like: *"I am safe. I am loved. I am enough."*

By practicing self-compassion, you replace judgment with acceptance and create a nurturing internal environment.

2. Establishing Safety and Structure - As children, we rely on routines and boundaries to create a sense of safety. Emotional neglect often means growing up without this consistency, leading to feelings of chaos or insecurity. Reparenting involves creating your own structure to foster safety and stability.

Practical Steps to Establish Structure:
- **Create Routines**: Develop daily routines that provide predictability and comfort. This can include a regular sleep schedule, meal times, or morning and evening rituals.
- **Set Boundaries**: Establish boundaries with others to protect your emotional and mental space. This might mean saying "no" when you need rest or limiting time with people who drain your energy.
- **Build Safe Spaces**: Designate spaces in your home that feel calming and secure. Surround yourself with objects or activities that bring comfort, such as cozy blankets, soft lighting, or relaxing hobbies.

Structure and safety help calm the nervous system and build trust with yourself, reinforcing that you are capable of providing the stability you need.

3. Creating Nurturing Self-Care Rituals - Self-care is an essential part of reparenting. It is the intentional practice of nurturing your emotional, physical, and mental well-being. For those who experienced emotional neglect, self-care may feel foreign or unimportant, but it is a way to show yourself the care and attention you deserve.

Self-Care Practices:
  - **Comfort and Play**: Engage in activities that bring you joy and relaxation, like painting, listening to music, spending time in nature, or playing games. These moments allow you to reconnect with your inner child.
  - **Emotional Release**: Make time to process emotions through journaling, therapy, or creative expression. Allow yourself to feel without judgment.
  - **Physical Care**: Treat your body with kindness through nourishing meals, gentle movement, and rest. Even small acts — like drinking water, stretching, or taking a warm bath — are ways to nurture yourself.

Self-care rituals are not indulgent; they are vital tools for emotional healing and a way to show yourself love and compassion.

The Long-Term Benefits of Reparenting

Reparenting is a gradual process, but the benefits are transformative. By caring for your inner child and meeting your emotional needs, you:

1. Develop a deeper sense of self-worth and self-trust.
2. Build emotional resilience and stability.
3. Learn to treat yourself with the love and validation you always deserved.
4. Create healthier, more fulfilling relationships based on mutual care and boundaries.

Reparenting helps you rewrite old narratives shaped by emotional neglect, replacing them with a foundation of self-love, safety, and compassion.

Moving Forward

Reparenting is a gift you give to yourself — the gift of care, love, and healing. While you cannot change the past, you have the power to meet your own needs in the present. By connecting with your inner child, practicing self-compassion, and creating routines that nurture your well-being, you take meaningful steps toward recovery.

This process may feel unfamiliar or uncomfortable at first, but with patience and commitment, you will discover the transformative power of reparenting. You are now the caregiver you needed — capable, loving, and devoted to creating the emotional safety and validation you always deserved.

Through reparenting, you reclaim your ability to thrive, heal, and embrace life as your truest self.

Chapter 8: Rebuilding Emotional Regulation

Emotional neglect leaves a lasting imprint on an individual's ability to recognize, express, and regulate emotions. When key emotional needs are unmet in childhood, many adults struggle to navigate their feelings, often suppressing or becoming overwhelmed by them. Rebuilding emotional regulation is a vital part of healing these wounds, as it allows individuals to connect with their emotions in healthier ways and respond to life's challenges with stability and confidence.

Understanding Emotional Regulation

Emotional regulation is the ability to understand, process, and manage emotions effectively. For those who experienced "Type A" trauma, this skill was often never taught or modeled. As children, emotions may have been dismissed, ignored, or invalidated, leaving individuals to believe that feelings were unwanted, unimportant, or unsafe. Over time, this leads to common patterns such as:

- **Suppressing emotions**: Bottling up feelings to avoid discomfort.
- **Overreacting**: Emotions surfacing as outbursts due to years of suppression.
- **Emotional numbness**: Feeling disconnected or detached from emotions entirely.
- **Overwhelm**: Struggling to cope when strong emotions arise.

Rebuilding emotional regulation means learning to identify your emotions, express them safely, and manage them in ways that support your overall well-being.

Learning Emotional Literacy

The first step in rebuilding emotional regulation is developing **emotional literacy**, which is the ability to recognize and name your emotions. Emotional literacy helps you move from feeling overwhelmed or confused to understanding what you are experiencing and why.

Steps to Build Emotional Literacy:
- **Name Your Emotions**: Instead of saying, *"I feel bad,"* try to be more specific. Are you sad, frustrated, anxious, or disappointed? Naming emotions helps you understand them better.
  - Use tools like an **emotion wheel** or a feelings chart to identify emotions.
- **Observe Without Judgment**: When emotions arise, practice observing them instead of labeling them as "good" or "bad." Emotions are simply information about your internal experience.
- **Reflect on Triggers**: Ask yourself: *"What happened to make me feel this way?"* Understanding your triggers helps you respond more intentionally.

For example, if you feel anger, take a moment to pause and identify the underlying emotion. Anger may mask hurt, sadness, or a sense of rejection. Developing this awareness empowers you to respond to emotions in a more informed and constructive way.

Tools for Managing Overwhelming Emotions

Learning to manage emotions requires practical techniques that help you stay grounded and calm when feelings become intense.

1. Mindfulness - Mindfulness involves bringing your attention to the present moment without judgment. It allows you to observe your emotions and physical sensations as they arise, creating space between feeling and reacting.

Mindfulness Practice:
- Sit comfortably and focus on your breath.
- When emotions arise, simply notice them: *"I am feeling anxious,"* or *"I am feeling sad."*
- Avoid trying to change the emotion—just allow it to exist.

- Return your focus to your breath, reminding yourself that emotions come and go like waves.

Mindfulness helps you respond to emotions with intention rather than reacting impulsively.

2. Grounding Exercises - Grounding techniques help you stay connected to the present moment when emotions feel overwhelming or when you begin to dissociate.

Grounding Techniques:
- **5-4-3-2-1 Exercise**: Identify 5 things you can see, 4 things you can touch, 3 things you hear, 2 things you can smell, and 1 thing you can taste.
- **Physical Movement**: Walk, stretch, or run cold water over your hands to reconnect with your body.
- **Sensory Objects**: Keep a small, comforting object nearby (like a smooth stone or soft fabric) to focus your attention when emotions escalate.

Grounding exercises help regulate intense feelings by anchoring you in the here and now.

3. Breathing Techniques - Intentional breathing calms the nervous system and reduces emotional overwhelm.

Example: Box Breathing
- Inhale slowly for 4 counts.
- Hold your breath for 4 counts.
- Exhale slowly for 4 counts.
- Hold again for 4 counts.

Repeat this cycle until you feel more centered and calm. Breathing exercises are simple yet powerful tools for emotional regulation.

The Role of Therapy in Emotional Healing
While mindfulness and grounding tools are effective, therapy plays a critical role in addressing the deeper emotional wounds

caused by "Type A" trauma. A trained therapist provides a safe space to explore emotions, identify patterns, and rebuild emotional regulation skills.

How Therapy Helps:
- **Processing Suppressed Emotions**: Therapy allows you to explore feelings that may have been buried for years. With guidance, you can grieve unmet needs, express emotions safely, and release unresolved pain.
- **Learning New Coping Skills**: Therapists can teach you techniques for managing emotions, building emotional awareness, and responding to triggers.
- **Reconnecting with Your Inner Child**: Many therapeutic approaches, such as inner child work, help you address the emotional needs that were neglected in childhood and provide the nurturing you deserved.
- **Building Emotional Safety**: A therapist models a healthy, supportive relationship, which helps you rebuild trust and learn to express emotions without fear of judgment.

Seeking therapy is a courageous step in reclaiming emotional health. It provides tools, insight, and support that can accelerate your healing journey.

Moving Toward Emotional Stability
Rebuilding emotional regulation takes time, patience, and practice. The goal is not to eliminate emotions but to learn how to experience, express, and manage them in ways that promote healing and balance.

Remember:
- Emotions are not your enemy. They are signals that guide you toward what you need.
- You are not "too emotional" or "broken" for feeling deeply. Your emotions are valid and deserve to be honored.

- Progress, not perfection, is the goal. Small steps toward emotional regulation — like pausing before reacting or naming your feelings — are signs of growth.

By developing emotional literacy, practicing mindfulness, using grounding tools, and seeking therapeutic support, you can rebuild emotional stability and resilience. Over time, you will learn to approach your emotions with understanding and compassion, creating space for a healthier, more fulfilling life.

Moving Forward
Rebuilding emotional regulation is a transformative part of healing from emotional neglect. As you learn to recognize, express, and manage your emotions, you reclaim the emotional balance that was denied in childhood.

With patience and consistent practice, you can navigate life's challenges with greater confidence, experience deeper connections, and embrace your full emotional range without fear. This process not only brings healing but also helps you reconnect with yourself in profound and meaningful ways.

Chapter 9: Building Healthy Relationships

Healthy relationships are essential for healing from "Type A" trauma. Emotional neglect often leaves individuals with trust issues, a fear of vulnerability, and patterns of emotional unavailability. Rebuilding the capacity for connection is a critical step in recovery, as relationships provide the emotional safety, support, and validation that may have been missing in childhood. Learning to trust, set boundaries, and cultivate reciprocal relationships ensures that emotional needs are met in a balanced and fulfilling way.

Overcoming Trust Issues

Emotional neglect teaches children that relationships are unreliable or unsafe. When caregivers fail to meet emotional needs, the message received is: *"You can't count on others to show up for you."* This belief often carries into adulthood, making it difficult to trust others with your emotions or needs.

Adults who experienced emotional neglect may:
- Keep others at a distance to avoid disappointment.
- Struggle to believe that others have their best interests at heart.
- Doubt their own worthiness of love, care, or attention.

Rebuilding Trust – Overcoming trust issues begins with recognizing that past experiences do not define all relationships. Trust is not built instantly; it is developed gradually through consistent actions and emotional safety. To begin:

- **Start Small**: Share small parts of yourself with trusted individuals and observe their responses. Look for consistency and care over time.
- **Challenge Old Beliefs**: Remind yourself that not everyone will fail to meet your needs. Healthy relationships exist, and you are worthy of them.
- **Practice Self-Trust**: Trusting others begins with trusting yourself — your feelings, instincts, and ability to make safe choices in relationships.

Trusting again is a courageous act, but it is also necessary to form the deep, meaningful connections that foster healing.

Facing the Fear of Vulnerability
For those who experienced emotional neglect, vulnerability can feel dangerous. As children, expressing emotions may have led to rejection, dismissal, or invalidation. To protect themselves, many adults learn to suppress emotions or avoid opening up entirely.

Yet, vulnerability is the foundation of true connection. It is the willingness to be seen as you are — your joys, fears, needs, and flaws — without the armor of perfection or self-protection.

Steps to Embrace Vulnerability
1. **Acknowledge the Fear**: Recognize that your fear of vulnerability is rooted in past experiences and is no longer needed to keep you safe.
2. **Take Small Risks**: Begin by sharing something honest with someone you trust — a thought, a feeling, or a small need. Allow yourself to experience their response.
3. **Practice Self-Compassion**: Remind yourself that it is okay to feel scared. Vulnerability is a strength, not a weakness.
4. **Choose Safe People**: Vulnerability should not be given to everyone. Build connections with those who show empathy, respect, and care.

Vulnerability deepens relationships and helps others see the real you. It is a necessary step in breaking patterns of emotional isolation.

Setting and Maintaining Healthy Boundaries
Boundaries are essential for creating emotional safety in relationships. They help define where you end and another person begins, ensuring that your needs, values, and limits are respected. For adults who experienced emotional neglect, boundaries can feel foreign or uncomfortable. You may fear

setting boundaries because it risks rejection, or you may not know where to begin.

What Healthy Boundaries Look Like
- Saying "no" without guilt.
- Asking for what you need without apology.
- Protecting your emotional and physical well-being.
- Recognizing when a relationship is draining or unhealthy.

Steps to Set Boundaries
1. **Identify Your Needs**: Reflect on what feels safe and comfortable for you. What do you need to feel respected and supported in a relationship?
2. **Communicate Clearly**: Express your boundaries in a calm, direct manner. For example: *"I need some time to myself this weekend,"* or *"I don't feel comfortable discussing that topic."*
3. **Be Consistent**: Upholding boundaries takes practice. Consistency helps reinforce your needs and teaches others how to respect them.
4. **Let Go of Guilt**: Setting boundaries is not selfish—it is self-care. Remind yourself that you have the right to protect your emotional space.

Boundaries allow you to engage in relationships without sacrificing your emotional health. They create mutual respect and provide the foundation for healthy, fulfilling connections.

Cultivating Reciprocal Relationships

Healthy relationships are reciprocal—they involve mutual care, respect, and emotional investment. For individuals who experienced emotional neglect, relationships may feel one-sided. You may give endlessly to others in hopes of being valued, or you may withhold affection, fearing rejection or hurt.

Reciprocal relationships require balance:
- **Give and Receive**: Allow yourself to both offer and accept support, love, and care.

- **Recognize Red Flags**: Be mindful of relationships where you feel consistently unheard, unseen, or taken advantage of.
- **Seek Emotional Safety**: Build relationships with people who honor your boundaries, validate your emotions, and show up consistently.

Nurturing Healthy Connections To cultivate reciprocal relationships:
- Prioritize people who show genuine care, consistency, and effort.
- Let go of relationships that are emotionally draining or one-sided.
- Be intentional about showing up for others while also allowing yourself to be seen and supported.

By choosing relationships that value balance and mutual emotional needs, you create a safe and fulfilling emotional environment that fosters healing.

Moving Forward: Building Connection and Safety
Healthy relationships are a vital part of recovery. Overcoming trust issues, embracing vulnerability, and setting boundaries are not easy tasks—but they are transformative. Through relationships, you can experience the emotional safety, love, and validation that may have been missing in your childhood.

It is okay to move slowly. Building healthy connections takes time, patience, and practice. Celebrate the small steps—sharing a piece of yourself, saying "no," or trusting someone a little more than before. Each effort brings you closer to relationships that nurture and uplift you.

You deserve relationships that honor your needs, value your presence, and offer emotional safety. By building these connections, you are not only healing the wounds of the past but also creating a future filled with trust, love, and fulfillment.

Chapter 10: Developing Emotional Intelligence – Emotional intelligence involves identifying, understanding, and regulating emotions, which are essential skills for healing. By improving emotional awareness, individuals can strengthen interpersonal relationships, fostering healthier and more fulfilling connections.

Chapter 11: Finding Meaning and Purpose – Healing involves transforming pain into personal growth. Exploring passions and core values helps rebuild a sense of identity and direction. Helping others becomes a powerful tool in the healing process, offering both meaning and fulfillment.

Chapter 12: Letting Go and Moving Forward – Healing is a lifelong journey that requires acceptance of imperfection and a focus on progress rather than perfection. Recognizing and celebrating milestones, both big and small, fosters motivation and reinforces the path toward wholeness.

Chapter 10: Developing Emotional Intelligence

Emotional intelligence is a critical component of healing from "Type A" trauma. It allows individuals to identify, understand, and regulate their emotions—skills that may not have been nurtured during childhood. For those who experienced emotional neglect, emotions were often ignored, dismissed, or invalidated, leaving them unequipped to manage their internal world effectively. Developing emotional intelligence is not only about improving self-awareness but also about fostering healthier, more fulfilling connections with others.

What is Emotional Intelligence?
Emotional intelligence (EI) is the ability to:
1. **Identify** your emotions and recognize what you are feeling.
2. **Understand** your emotions, including why they arise and what they mean.
3. **Regulate** your emotions by managing them in healthy and constructive ways.
4. **Recognize emotions in others** to build empathy and meaningful connections.
5. **Respond effectively** to emotions, both in yourself and in your relationships.

While emotional intelligence may seem like an innate ability for some, it is a skill that can be developed and strengthened with practice. By cultivating EI, you empower yourself to navigate emotions with confidence, improve your well-being, and create deeper, more satisfying relationships.

Identifying Your Emotions
The first step in developing emotional intelligence is learning to identify your emotions. For those who grew up with emotional neglect, feelings may have been suppressed or ignored to the point where they feel unfamiliar or overwhelming. You may struggle to name what you're feeling, leaving you disconnected from your emotional experience.

Steps to Identify Emotions:
- **Pause and Reflect**: When you feel something, pause and ask yourself, *"What am I feeling right now?"*
- **Use Emotion Words**: Expand your emotional vocabulary beyond basic terms like "sad" or "angry." Use tools like an **emotion wheel** to help you pinpoint more nuanced feelings such as "disappointed," "frustrated," or "lonely."
- **Check Your Body**: Emotions often show up in physical sensations.

For example:
- Tight shoulders might signal stress.
- A lump in your throat could indicate sadness.
- A fluttering in your stomach may reflect anxiety.

When you consistently identify and name your emotions, you create a bridge between your internal experience and your awareness, fostering greater emotional clarity.

Understanding Your Emotions

Once you identify what you're feeling, the next step is understanding why those emotions are present. Emotional neglect often disconnects people from the *"why"* behind their feelings, leaving emotions unprocessed and misunderstood.

Ways to Understand Your Emotions:
- **Ask Questions**: Reflect on what triggered the emotion:
  - *"What happened to make me feel this way?"*
  - *"What does this emotion tell me about my needs or boundaries?"*
- **Look for Patterns**: Notice recurring emotional responses. For example, does anger arise when you feel unheard? Does sadness emerge when you feel disconnected from others? Recognizing patterns helps you understand the deeper roots of your emotions.
- **Acknowledge Without Judgment**: Allow yourself to feel emotions without labeling them as "good" or

"bad." Instead, remind yourself: *"This is my body and mind responding to something important."*

Understanding your emotions empowers you to respond to them effectively rather than feeling controlled by them.

Regulating Your Emotions
Emotional regulation is the ability to manage your emotions in ways that are constructive and balanced. For individuals who experienced "Type A" trauma, emotional regulation may feel challenging because they were never taught how to process or cope with strong emotions. Instead of reacting impulsively or avoiding feelings altogether, emotional regulation involves responding with intention and care.

Techniques to Regulate Emotions:

1. **Mindfulness**
   a. Focus on the present moment to observe your emotions without becoming overwhelmed.
   b. Practice breathing exercises to calm your nervous system. For example:
   c. *Inhale for 4 counts, hold for 4 counts, and exhale for 4 counts.*
2. **Grounding Exercises**
   a. Use grounding techniques to calm intense emotions. Try the *5-4-3-2-1 method:*
   b. Identify 5 things you can see, 4 things you can touch, 3 things you hear, 2 things you smell, and 1 thing you taste.
3. **Journaling**
   a. Writing about your emotions helps you process and release them. Reflect on what you're feeling and why.
4. **Healthy Outlets**
   a. Channel emotions into physical activity, creative expression, or self-soothing practices. Examples include walking, painting, listening to music, or simply resting.

By regulating emotions, you reduce impulsive reactions and create space to respond thoughtfully, leading to better outcomes for yourself and your relationships.

Strengthening Interpersonal Relationships
Emotional intelligence doesn't stop with understanding yourself; it extends to how you connect with others. Healthy relationships rely on empathy, emotional awareness, and clear communication — all of which are strengthened through EI.

Ways to Foster Healthier Connections:

1. **Practice Active Listening**: Give others your full attention. Reflect on their emotions and respond with empathy. For example: *"It sounds like you're feeling really overwhelmed right now. Is there something I can do to help?"*
2. **Express Your Emotions Clearly**: Communicate your feelings and needs honestly but respectfully. For example: *"I felt hurt when I wasn't included in the conversation because connection is really important to me."*
3. **Recognize Emotional Cues**: Pay attention to non-verbal signals in others, such as tone, body language, or facial expressions, to better understand their emotions.
4. **Show Empathy**: Empathy involves stepping into someone else's experience without judgment. Practice asking questions like: *"How did that make you feel?"* or offering supportive affirmations like: *"That sounds really hard."*

When you strengthen your ability to understand and connect with others emotionally, you build trust, deepen relationships, and create healthier, more fulfilling bonds.

Moving Forward: Emotional Intelligence for Lifelong Growth
Developing emotional intelligence is an ongoing process. By improving your ability to identify, understand, and regulate your emotions, you equip yourself with tools to navigate life with resilience and self-awareness. Emotional intelligence

becomes the bridge that allows you to connect with yourself and others more authentically.

Key Takeaways:
1. Emotional intelligence starts with self-awareness: identify and name your emotions.
2. Understanding your emotions helps you process and respond to them intentionally.
3. Regulating emotions allows you to remain calm, centered, and constructive in challenging situations.
4. Strengthening emotional connections with others fosters trust, empathy, and deeper relationships.

As you build emotional intelligence, you not only heal from the wounds of emotional neglect but also develop a skill set that empowers you to live a more connected, fulfilling life. Remember, every step you take — whether it's naming a feeling, managing a difficult emotion, or showing empathy to someone else — reinforces your emotional growth.

Emotional intelligence is the foundation for creating healthier relationships with yourself and others. With practice and patience, it becomes a guiding force, allowing you to experience life with greater understanding, connection, and purpose.

Chapter 11: Finding Meaning and Purpose

Healing from "Type A" trauma—emotional neglect—extends beyond addressing wounds and rebuilding emotional health. A critical part of the journey is finding meaning and purpose in your experiences. When pain is transformed into personal growth, it becomes a source of strength and direction rather than a weight that holds you back. By exploring your passions, identifying your core values, and helping others, you can rebuild a sense of identity and discover fulfillment that supports long-term healing.

Transforming Pain into Growth

The pain of emotional neglect can feel overwhelming and isolating, but it also holds the potential for transformation. Many individuals who heal from emotional wounds find that their struggles give them a unique perspective, resilience, and the capacity for deep empathy.

Rather than denying or dismissing the pain of what was missing, personal growth comes from asking:

- *"What have my experiences taught me?"*
- *"How can I use this pain to grow stronger, wiser, or more connected?"*
- *"What do I want my life to look like now that I'm choosing to heal?"*

Transforming pain doesn't mean invalidating the hurt or pretending it no longer matters. Instead, it means acknowledging its impact, honoring how it shaped you, and intentionally using it as a foundation to build a life of meaning and purpose.

Exploring Your Passions and Values

For many adults who experienced emotional neglect, their sense of identity may feel underdeveloped or unclear. Without emotional support or guidance as children, they may have learned to suppress their interests, ignore their needs, or shape themselves to fit others' expectations. Rediscovering your passions and core values is an essential part of reconnecting with yourself.

Identifying Your Passions

Passions are activities, ideas, or pursuits that bring you joy, energy, and a sense of purpose.

To uncover your passions:
- **Reflect on Joy**: Ask yourself, *"What activities make me lose track of time?"* or *"What did I love to do as a child?"* This could include art, writing, nature, music, helping others, or exploring new ideas.
- **Experiment**: Give yourself permission to try new things without pressure. Take a class, pick up a hobby, or reconnect with old interests to see what excites you.
- **Notice What Energizes You**: Pay attention to moments when you feel most alive or fulfilled, whether it's connecting with people, creating something, or learning a new skill.

Clarifying Your Core Values

Core values are the principles that guide your decisions, actions, and sense of purpose. Identifying these values helps you align your life with what truly matters to you.

To clarify your values:
- Reflect on moments when you felt proud, fulfilled, or connected. What values were present? (e.g., kindness, creativity, honesty, growth, or connection.)
- Ask yourself, *"What kind of person do I want to be?"* and *"What do I want my life to stand for?"*
- Write a list of your top 3-5 values and use them to guide your choices and priorities.

When you align your passions and values, you build a sense of direction and identity. This alignment becomes a compass that helps you make choices rooted in meaning rather than fear or survival.

Helping Others: Healing Through Service
One of the most powerful ways to find meaning and purpose is
to help others. Sharing your experiences, offering support, or
contributing to causes you care about can turn your pain into a
source of empowerment—for both yourself and those you help.

Helping others creates:
- **Connection**: By showing up for others, you build
  meaningful relationships that combat isolation and
  deepen empathy.
- **Fulfillment**: Helping others brings a sense of purpose,
  showing you that your struggles have value and can
  make a difference.
- **Healing**: Offering support to others can help you
  reparent yourself by providing the care and
  encouragement you may have needed as a child.

Ways to Help Others:
- **Share Your Story**: Whether through writing, speaking,
  or conversations, sharing your journey can inspire and
  validate others who are struggling.
- **Volunteer**: Get involved with causes that align with
  your values, such as mental health advocacy,
  community service, or mentoring programs.
- **Support Loved Ones**: Show up with empathy and
  understanding for friends or family members
  navigating their own challenges.

Helping others doesn't mean neglecting your own needs. It's
about using your growth to give back in a way that also
nourishes you.

Rebuilding Your Identity
Healing from emotional neglect often requires rediscovering
who you are outside of your past experiences. Rebuilding your
identity involves exploring questions like:

- *"What brings me joy and fulfillment?"*
- *"What are my strengths, and how can I use them to build a meaningful life?"*
- *"What kind of relationships do I want to nurture?"*

Start small and celebrate each step as you reconnect with yourself:

- Create a life that reflects your values and passions.
- Pursue goals that matter to you, not ones defined by others.
- Build relationships that honor your needs and encourage your growth.

Rebuilding your identity allows you to move beyond the pain of what was missing and embrace the potential of what you can create.

Moving Forward: A Life of Meaning and Purpose
Finding meaning and purpose is about reclaiming control over your story. While you cannot change the past, you can choose how to live in the present and build a future that aligns with your truth.

- **Honor Your Journey**: Recognize the strength it takes to transform pain into growth and acknowledge how far you've come.
- **Stay Curious**: Healing and growth are lifelong processes. Continue to explore what brings you fulfillment and meaning as you evolve.
- **Create Your Own Legacy**: Whether through small acts of kindness, creativity, or service, your life has value and purpose.

By exploring your passions, aligning with your values, and helping others, you transform the void left by emotional neglect into a foundation for connection, growth, and fulfillment. Your pain does not define you — it shapes the strength, resilience, and compassion you carry forward.

Final Thoughts
Finding meaning and purpose is not a destination but a journey of self-discovery. It's about choosing to transform pain into something greater and creating a life that reflects who you truly are. When you embrace this process, you not only heal yourself but also inspire others to do the same.

Your story matters. Your growth matters. And your life has meaning — far beyond what you once believed possible. By moving forward with intention and purpose, you reclaim your power and open yourself to a future filled with possibility, connection, and fulfillment.

Chapter 12: Letting Go and Moving Forward

Healing from "Type A" trauma—emotional neglect—is not a destination but a lifelong journey. The process of addressing emotional wounds, rebuilding your sense of self, and fostering healthier relationships takes time, patience, and compassion. Along the way, you'll encounter setbacks and breakthroughs, moments of doubt and moments of growth. Moving forward requires letting go of perfection, embracing progress, and learning to celebrate every step you take toward wholeness.

Acceptance of Imperfection
One of the greatest challenges in the healing process is learning to accept imperfection—in yourself, in others, and in the journey itself. For many adults who experienced emotional neglect, perfectionism became a survival strategy. You may have believed that if you worked hard enough, behaved perfectly, or never showed vulnerability, you could earn the love, validation, and safety you craved.

However, perfectionism only reinforces feelings of inadequacy. The reality is that healing is messy, nonlinear, and full of imperfections. Accepting this truth is freeing because it allows you to shift your focus away from unrealistic expectations and toward self-compassion and progress.

Ways to Embrace Imperfection:
- **Let Go of "Shoulds"**: Replace thoughts like *"I should be further along,"* with *"I am doing my best, and that is enough."*
- **Be Gentle with Setbacks**: Healing isn't a straight line. When you face setbacks, remind yourself that they are part of the process, not a failure.
- **Celebrate Effort, Not Perfection**: Progress is found in the effort you put forth, even if the outcome isn't perfect. Each step, no matter how small, is significant.

By embracing imperfection, you allow yourself to grow at your own pace and discover the beauty of being human—flaws and all.

Focusing on Progress, Not Perfection
Healing requires shifting your focus from perfection to progress. Progress is not about achieving an ideal version of yourself but about moving toward greater emotional awareness, connection, and resilience. Some days, progress might look like naming your emotions or setting a small boundary. Other days, it might be recognizing an old pattern and choosing a new, healthier response.

Signs of Progress to Celebrate:
1. You respond to overwhelming emotions with greater calm or clarity.
2. You recognize and name your feelings instead of suppressing them.
3. You set a boundary, even if it feels uncomfortable.
4. You allow yourself to grieve or feel without judgment.
5. You trust someone enough to share a vulnerable part of yourself.

No step is too small to celebrate. Progress happens in moments of awareness, intentional choices, and the quiet victories that often go unnoticed. Acknowledging these milestones reinforces the path you're on and motivates you to keep moving forward.

Recognizing and Celebrating Milestones
Healing from emotional neglect is a courageous act, and every milestone deserves to be honored. Too often, individuals dismiss their achievements, focusing instead on what's still left to do. Celebrating your progress, both big and small, helps you recognize how far you've come and reinforces your commitment to healing.

Ideas for Celebrating Milestones:
- **Reflect on Growth**: Take time to look back and write about the ways you've grown. Reflect on the changes you've made and the challenges you've overcome.
- **Treat Yourself**: Celebrate milestones with meaningful rewards, like taking yourself out for a favorite meal, enjoying a quiet day of self-care, or buying something special to mark your progress.
- **Share Your Wins**: Share your achievements with a trusted friend, therapist, or support group. Allow others to celebrate with you.
- **Create a Progress Jar**: Write down moments of progress on slips of paper and place them in a jar. Over time, you'll have a visual reminder of your growth.

Celebrating milestones fosters motivation, builds confidence, and reminds you that healing is happening—even when it doesn't always feel like it.

Letting Go of What No Longer Serves You
Moving forward requires letting go—letting go of old patterns, outdated beliefs, and the pain that no longer serves you. This doesn't mean forgetting the past or dismissing your experiences. Instead, it's about releasing the hold they have on you.

What You Can Let Go Of:
1. The belief that you are unworthy of love, connection, or care.
2. The need for perfection or external validation to feel "enough."
3. Resentment toward those who failed to meet your emotional needs.
4. Patterns of people-pleasing, avoidance, or emotional suppression.

Letting go is an act of self-liberation. It allows you to create space for growth, self-compassion, and the relationships you truly deserve.

Moving Forward with Intention
Letting go and moving forward does not mean leaving the past behind completely—it means learning from it, honoring your story, and building a future based on your truth. As you continue your healing journey, approach it with intention:

- **Practice Patience**: Healing is not a race. Trust that you are exactly where you need to be.
- **Stay Curious**: Remain open to learning about yourself, your emotions, and your needs. Healing is a process of discovery.
- **Prioritize Self-Compassion**: Treat yourself with kindness, especially on hard days. You deserve the same care and understanding you give others.

A Lifelong Journey Toward Wholeness
Healing from emotional neglect is a lifelong process, but each step brings you closer to wholeness. By letting go of perfection, focusing on progress, and celebrating milestones, you create a foundation of self-trust, emotional resilience, and fulfillment.

You cannot change the past, but you can choose how to move forward. Every moment of awareness, every boundary set, and every act of self-compassion is a victory. Healing is not about achieving perfection—it's about learning to live authentically, love yourself unconditionally, and create the life you deserve.

As you continue this journey, remind yourself:
- *"I am healing at my own pace."*
- *"I am proud of how far I've come."*
- *"I am worthy of love, care, and wholeness."*

Letting go and moving forward is an ongoing act of courage. You have already taken the most important step—you've begun. Celebrate that, and keep going. Your journey toward healing and wholeness is worth every effort.

Conclusion

The Power of Healing

The journey through "Type A" trauma is one of profound self-discovery, grief, and growth. From understanding the silent wounds of emotional neglect to grieving the losses of a childhood that lacked love, validation, and safety, the process of healing begins with acknowledgment. By breaking the silence and validating our own experiences, we reclaim the parts of ourselves that were unseen and unheard.

Addressing these wounds requires courage and commitment. Reparenting our inner child, rebuilding emotional regulation, and forming healthy relationships allow us to nurture the emotional safety and connection we always deserved. These steps remind us that it is never too late to meet our needs, rewrite our patterns, and foster meaningful, reciprocal bonds.

Moving toward wholeness is a lifelong process—one that requires patience, self-compassion, and acceptance of imperfection. By developing emotional intelligence, finding meaning in our struggles, and transforming pain into purpose, we create opportunities for growth, resilience, and joy. Celebrating milestones along the way, no matter how small, is a testament to our progress and strength.

Healing is not about erasing the past but about embracing vulnerability, connection, and the power of self-love. It is a journey of reclaiming what was lost and creating a life of authenticity, purpose, and fulfillment.

Remember, it is never too late to heal from the silent wounds of "Type A" trauma. You are worthy of love, belonging, and wholeness—no matter where your story began. Your journey is not defined by what you lacked but by the steps you take to rebuild, reclaim, and thrive.

NOTES

Here is a curated list of resources to enhance the content of your book on Type A Trauma. These resources are organized into categories such as books, articles, tools, organizations, and therapeutic approaches, offering readers practical guidance and opportunities for deeper exploration.

Books

1. "Running on Empty" by Dr. Jonice Webb - Focuses on understanding childhood emotional neglect and strategies for healing.
2. "Adult Children of Emotionally Immature Parents" by Lindsay C. Gibson - Explores the impact of emotionally neglectful parenting on adulthood and how to recover.
3. "The Deepest Well" by Dr. Nadine Burke Harris - Examines how childhood trauma impacts lifelong health and provides steps for healing.
4. "Waking the Tiger" by Peter A. Levine - Discusses trauma's effects on the body and offers somatic approaches for healing.
5. "It Didn't Start With You" by Mark Wolynn - Explores inherited family trauma and its impact on mental health and behavior.

Articles & Research

1. National Child Traumatic Stress Network (NCTSN) - Offers articles on trauma, its effects, and resources for recovery.
2. Harvard Center on the Developing Child - Research on how early emotional experiences shape brain development.
3. Psychology Today: Emotional Neglect - Practical insights and advice from mental health professionals on managing emotional neglect.

Self-Help Tools

1. Journaling Prompts
   - Example: Write about a time you felt unseen as a child. How does that memory affect you today?

• Use these prompts for Chapter 6's guided exercises.
2. Emotion Wheel
   • Helps readers recognize and name their emotions for Chapter 8 on emotional literacy.
3. Self-Compassion Practices
   • Use Dr. Kristin Neff's self-compassion exercises to supplement Chapter 7.

Online Courses & Videos

1. Healing Childhood Emotional Neglect (Dr. Jonice Webb's Online Course) - Provides structured modules for understanding and recovering from emotional neglect.
2. Mindfulness-Based Stress Reduction (MBSR) Courses - Available online to help readers build emotional regulation skills.
3. TED Talks: Brené Brown - Talks on vulnerability and emotional resilience align with Chapters 5 and 9.

Therapeutic Approaches

1. Internal Family Systems (IFS) Therapy - Helps with reparenting (Chapter 7) and emotional regulation (Chapter 8).
2. Somatic Experiencing (SE) - Focuses on releasing trauma stored in the body, supplementing Chapter 8.
3. Attachment-Based Therapy - Addresses relationship challenges discussed in Chapter 9.

Apps

1. Headspace or Calm - Mindfulness apps for grounding and emotional regulation exercises (Chapter 8).
2. MoodPath - Tracks emotional well-being and provides journaling prompts.
3. Woebot - A chatbot that provides emotional support and cognitive behavioral therapy techniques.

<u>**Organizations**</u>

1. Childhood Emotional Neglect Project (CEN) - Offers resources and community support for individuals recovering from emotional neglect.
2. The Trauma Recovery Institute - Provides articles, courses, and webinars on healing trauma.
3. National Alliance on Mental Illness (NAMI) - Support groups and resources for navigating mental health challenges related to trauma.

<u>**Worksheets & Printables**</u>

1. Boundaries Worksheet
   - Guides on identifying, setting, and maintaining healthy boundaries (Chapter 9).
   - Available for free download from therapy websites like TherapistAid.com.
2. Grief Workbooks
   - Support Chapter 6 by guiding readers through the grieving process.
3. Emotion Regulation Worksheets
   - Printable tools to help readers practice mindfulness, grounding, and self-awareness.

<u>**Support Groups**</u>

1. Adult Children of Alcoholics (ACOA) or Dysfunctional Families - Support groups for individuals recovering from childhood neglect and trauma.
2. Online Trauma Recovery Groups (via Meetup or Reddit) - Safe spaces for connecting with others who share similar experiences.

<u>**Other Titles Available**</u>

- Finding Hope in God's Word as Survivors of Childhood Trauma: Therapeutic Devotional

- Therapeutic Journal Prompts: 10 Subjects, Over 300 Prompts

- 90 Days - Developing a Deeper Relationship with God

- You Don't Know What You Don't Know...: Quick Reads #4

- The Worth Within: 10 Practices to Transform Your Life and Reclaim Your Confidence

- Decision Making with God in Mind: A process in helping alleviate anxiety and hopelessness

- Lights in the Darkness - Reparenting Yourself after Childhood Trauma

- It's Not About Blame but Understanding: Healing the Hurts of the Past

- Finding Freedom in Love: Untangling Mother's Expectations and God's Grace

- Parenting Teens and Young Adults - Workbook: (...reducing the likelihood of failure to launch)